It was a cold, wet night
and the wind was blowing a gale.
An old man was walking slowly along the road.
He was wet, cold, tired and hungry,
for he had walked a very long way.
Suddenly, he came upon a house,
so he went up and knocked on the door.
A cook opened the door and the old man asked the cook
if she would give him some food,
but the cook told him that she had none.
"May I come in and dry myself by the fire, then?"
asked the old man.
"All right," said the cook, "but you mustn't get in my way."

2   So the old man went in and sat down by the fire.
Soon he was warm, dry and not so tired,
but he still felt very hungry.
After a while he said to the cook,
"I am a very good cook myself.
I can make a beautiful soup. It is called stone soup."
The cook, who prided herself on being an excellent cook,
had never heard of stone soup.
She wanted very much to know
how to make such a cheap soup,
so she asked the old man
to show her how it was made.

The old man got up from the fireside
and began to make the stone soup.
"Get me a large pot with some water in it,"
he asked the cook.
When the cook brought this, he put it over the fire.
Then he took a smooth white stone from his pocket
and dropped it into the pot of water.

4

After a while the water was hot
and the old man took a spoon and tasted the soup.
"This is going to be delicious soup,
but it needs a few vegetables added
to give it a little more flavor.
I see that old piece of cabbage
and a few onions on the table over there.
May I drop them in?"
The cook, who was watching everything that the old man did,
nodded, and in went the vegetables.

After a while the old man tasted the soup again and said,
"Mmmm, this is going to be really delicious,
but it needs a little stirring.
Would you mind if I used that ham bone over there
to stir the soup?"
Again the cook nodded and
the old man began to stir the soup with the ham bone.

6

After a further time the old man tasted the soup again
and said, "Mmmm, this soup is going to be really, really delicious,
but I think that it needs a little flour to thicken it.
Would you have a little flour?"
The cook got him some flour
and the old man put it into the soup,
stirring it all the time.
After a further time the old man tasted the soup again
and said, "Mmmmm, this is really going to be the best soup
I have ever made.

A little bit of butter and a drop of cream
would make it perfect."
So the cook got up
to get the old man the butter and the cream.
"While you are getting those," said the old man,
"pass me that chicken I can see. It can't do any harm."
So in went the butter, the cream and the chicken,
and the old man stirred and stirred
the stone soup with the ham bone.

8

After a little while he tasted the soup again and said,
"Mmmmm, this is really the most delicious soup
I have ever made.
It is fit for a King or a Queen."
So he poured out some soup,
some for the cook and some for himself.
He fished out the stone from the soup,
wiped it clean and put it back in his pocket.
"This is really delicious soup," said the cook.
"It's the best soup I have ever had,
and to think that it was made from a stone!
I am so glad that I have learned to make stone soup."